T0208342

CRACK BABY

Nyree Watkins

authorHOUSE®

AuthorHouse™
1663 Liberty Drive
Bloomington, IN 47403
www.authorhouse.com
Phone: 833-262-8899

Published by AuthorHouse 04/22/2021

ISBN: 978-1-6655-2375-2 (sc)
ISBN: 978-1-6655-2376-9 (hc)
ISBN: 978-1-6655-2385-1 (e)

Library of Congress Control Number: 2021908368

Print information available on the last page.

Remember, the struggles along the way are only meant to shape you for your purpose.

—Chadwick Boseman

CONTENTS

ACKNOWLEDGEMENTS

First, I would like to thank God for making all things possible in my life.

I thank my daughters, Mo'Nyra, Tori, Naomi, and Abigail, for keeping mommy on her toes and helping me become the best version of myself.

I thank my Aunt Jeanette for being my backbone and for loving me unconditionally.

I thank my cousin Nike, my Aunt Cotchie, and my Aunt Renee for supporting me and encouraging me.

I thank my sister, Toiya Howard, for showing me how to work hard.

I thank my parents, Melinda Lindsay and Abdus Luqman, for always believing in me.

THE BEGINNING

Crack baby

My name is Nyree Dominique Watkins. I was born on February 26, 1988, at Saint Luke's Hospital in Cleveland, Ohio. I was not like the average baby because my mom smoked crack with me during her pregnancy. I had a few birth defects, which caused my eyes to roll in the back of my head. I would have fits and cry for long periods. I was a very unstable baby, mentally and physically.

My mom and dad were like Bonnie and Clyde. They had a crazy love. They tried to be there for me the best they could, but their addiction to crack cocaine often got in the way. Then, when I was one years old, my dad was sentenced to fifteen years in prison for robbery and my mom was sentenced to one year in prison for violating probation. Since my parents were in prison, I lived with my aunt Jeanette.

Aunt Jeanette was my mom's oldest sister and she had one son of her own. She was a realist and spoke truth. She loved hard and was one of our family's greatest supporters. Even though my aunt was struggling with her own drug addiction, she still made sure I was straight. I would often cry a lot. One night, I was crying uncontrollably. My aunt said she tried everything to stop me from crying and nothing worked, until she decided to blow crack smoke into the room I was crying in. She said I became so calm, and immediately she knew I was a crack baby.

After one year of living with my aunt, I went back to live with my mom once she was released from prison. My mom still chose to do drugs and would do practically anything to get high. She would turn tricks right in front of me. She would leave me with people she barely knew. Things got so bad that at one point, I remember licking barbeque sauce from an empty takeout box that had barbeque chicken in it days before. My mom couldn't feed both me and her drug addiction anymore. My mom was unable to take care of me, which meant that I moved back and forth between different family and friends frequently.

School #1

When I turned five, I was ready to start school for the first time. I attended kindergarten at Anthony Wayne Elementary. My Aunt Jeanette was taking care of me at my grandma's house at the time. A lot of people called my grandma "Virg," but her real name was Virginia. She was down-to-earth and would feed anybody. She would cuss you out and feed you all at the same time. She loved playing cards and going to bingo a few days a week. Grandma kept the family together. I had one sister on my mother's side and I was the only child on my father's side. My grandma always took care of my sister, even before I was born. I was a little jealous of the relationship they had because my sister got to stay with Grandma and didn't have to move around as much as I did.

School #2

When I was six years old, my mom went to rehab. After completing rehab, my mom felt she could take care of me and my sister. So, I went to live with my mom and attended Louis Pasture Elementary. We lived on Parkwood off East 105th street. Around this time, the hip hop group Bone Thugs-N-Harmony was popular, and the neighborhood they grew up in was just a few minutes away from our house. "It's the first of the month wake up, wake up, wake up. It's the first of the month, get up, get up, get up. So, cash yo checks and get up." Man, I loved that song.

My mom was working, and she was happy. She even had a boyfriend named Paul. He seemed very nice. He had a very distinctive laugh, and I could not help but laugh when he laughed. He was financially stable and would take me, my mom, and my sister on road trips from time to time. I remember our first road trip to Sandusky, Ohio. I will never forget that road trip because I burned my index finger from the car lighter in Paul's van. That's what I get for being curious, I suppose. I had a circular scar on my finger for a whole month.

A couple of months later, I walked home from school to find my aunt Jeanette and Paul in the driveway. Aunt Jeanette hugged me and told me she was taking me with her because my mom was sick and that she couldn't take care of my sister and me any longer. I started crying. I felt like my life was just beginning, with my own bedroom, a new home, and a new school. I was confused and I didn't understand why my aunt and my mother's boyfriend were telling me my mom was sick. My mom wasn't coughing or acting strange, from what I could tell, so what kind of sickness were they talking about? Where was my mother? Why did I have to live with my aunt again? I did not understand. And again, my sister and I had to part ways. She went to my grandma's house, and I went with my aunt.

School #3: Anger

My aunt was staying with my big cousin Nike at that point. I moved in with them in the Park Place Apartments on Wade Park. I was to attend Sunbeam Elementary with my big cousin's daughter. I did not want to go. I was stubborn and embarrassed because I didn't know anybody but my cousin Nunu, and she wasn't even in my class because she was in a higher grade. Back at my cousin house, I had to get used to sharing a bedroom with my cousin and sleeping in the same bed with her. I was so uncomfortable. I missed my own room. I missed my sister and my mom.

My big cousin Nike and my aunt Jeanette tried their best to take my mind off the situation. They could tell how angry and upset I was. As the days went by, things did get a little better. My cousin and I would play with our baby dolls together. Nike did not like to cook, so we often ate Taco Bell and barbecue from the trailer down the street. I started to get used to living with my cousins.

My big cousin Nike was gorgeous. She had it all together, in my eyes. She expressed love to me in a way that was heartfelt; her hugs were so full of love and warmth. I used to enjoy watching her get dressed. She would play R&B music and look in the mirror and sing while putting on her clothes, makeup, and perfume. Just watching her made me feel for music again. I would tune the radio to 93.1 and sing all the R&B songs I wanted. My love for music was coming back. It felt good to be back in motion, dancing and shimmying to music. I loved me some Whitney Houston, Michael Jackson, and Mary J. Blidge.

Music was my therapy, especially when I got angry. And I was often angry. I struggled with uncontrollable anger because of all the disappointments and instability in my life. I would get mad about the smallest things. The first time I really noticed my anger was when my cousin and I were playing with our baby dolls and I didn't get what I wanted, and so I threw the doll. Another time, I was making up the bed and the sheets were going in the wrong direction, so I bunched up the pillows and sheets and messed up the whole bed. My cousin NuNu would laugh at me all the time for my anger issues. I really didn't think it was funny, but it tickled her to see me so riled up. I guess it's safe to say I was still dealing with the issues that come with being born a crack baby.

School #4: Abandonment

My aunt and I ended up moving into my grandma's house again because she was having some personal issues and did not want to live with my big cousin anymore. Since my grandma's house was on the other side of town, I had to transfer to Alexander Graham Bell Elementary.

I started really missing my parents. I was sad and curious, and I began asking my aunt a lot of questions. "Auntie, is my mom coming back?" "Will I ever get to meet my dad?" I remember just crying and not understanding why my cousins and friends all had their moms, but mine was gone. I couldn't understand why my friends had their dads, but mine was gone. I was starting to think it was my fault. For the first time, I felt truly abandoned by my own parents. My aunt would tell me, "Nyree, baby, just keep your head up. Everything is going to be alright. Your mom will be back and soon you will see your father." No matter how my aunt tried to console me, I needed them now and they weren't there.

I remember picture days and daddy-and-daughter walks at school, and me showing up all alone. I was so angry. I would sing to take my mind off the situation. Singing was a way of escape. I felt like I was in another world when I sang. I would sing about anything. I started to dance and sing at my family gatherings and on holidays. To hear the clapping and applause from my family helped me take my mind off the absence of my parents. I knew I could sing and dance, but receiving confirmation from my family gave me confidence. One of my uncles once said it looked like I didn't have any bones from the way I would pop my body and do the splits.

I also remember certain people in my family would say negative things about the way I danced, but that didn't stop me. I was only a kid, and that was the way I expressed myself. Young as I was, I knew I was being judged, and so I started to pay attention to everything. They also judged me because my mom was on drugs and because I didn't have the nicest clothes to wear. Older aunts and uncles would talk, thinking I was too young to really understand, but what they didn't know was that their words planted a negative seed in my mind. I was only nine years old and their opinions were very important to me. I started to have a bad attitude because of the things I heard certain family members say about me and my mom. "Where her momma at?" "Why she keeps leaving her daughter?"

I became insecure about myself. I really felt like an outcast. People's words hurt me, and it hurt the most when those people were my own family. I was already dealing with anger issues and being judge didn't make things any better. My anger got so bad that certain family members didn't want to be around me because I would start speaking my mind, saying all sorts of nasty things out of hurt, sadness, and most of all anger.

School #5: First time meeting my dad

I turned ten and was in the fourth grade at Paul Revere Elementary. The summer was approaching. My mom had just finished another rehab program. My sister and I moved back in with my mom. I had missed the feeling of having my own room again. Since my mom knew I had talent, she put me in the Rainy Institute summer program where I got to explore performance arts, music, and arts and crafts. I loved it. She also signed me up for Showagon, the city's traveling performing arts troupe. It provided an opportunity for youth to show their talents at different venues throughout the city of Cleveland.

Thriving Moment

I was so excited about Showagon. The program provided four voice trainers to coach each talent. I had a great voice trainer. We chose the song "Angel of Mine" by the R&B artist Monica. When I performed that song, I became the fullest version of myself. I put my all into that song. I was also doing a dance duo with one of the guys on the show named Carl. He was much older than I was, but he could dance his butt off. We danced a duo to "Are you that somebody" by Aaliyah. When I tell you, we had the best dance performance in the show, I'm not bragging or exaggerating--we really did. Our bodies were in harmony, and we rocked the show. I danced like there was no tomorrow. I sang my song like there was no one listening. When I was on stage, I was where I belonged, performing. I felt so free. I had finally tapped into my gift of music.

When the summer programs came to an end, my mom allowed me to sign up for the drill team at my school. She also let me join the choir at Woodhill Recreation Center down the street. Later, I signed up to play basketball and volleyball, and I was pretty good at both. My mom made sure she kept me busy, and I loved all the activities.

My sister had her friends, and I had mine. My two best friends were a boy and a girl, George and Chalana. We did almost everything together. Chalana was my girl. We played basketball and volleyball together. George played basketball for the boys' team and I played basketball for the girls' team at Woodhill Recreation Center. I was really starting to have a normal life. I still struggled with my anger and if things didn't go my way, I would throw a fit behind closed doors. I did not like how anger had so much control over me.

Being a crack baby affected me in so many ways. I knew my anger was a problem, and I tried to hide because I felt embarrassed. I still turned to music for comfort when I felt angry or sad, and that helped a lot. Some of my family members and friends knew I had an anger problem, but I don't think they knew how bad it was. I hid my fits well, but I could not hide my fighting.

I remember getting into a fight at school with this new girl because she kept staring at me. I asked her what she was looking at, and she said something smart. So I smacked her in the face right there on the playground, and we started fighting. If I got offended in any way, I would fight. Anger was my kryptonite. My anger problem cost me a lot of friendships. I remember my mom punishing me a few times because of how I was acting in school. I liked to stay busy because it kept my anger at bay and kept me out of trouble.

I finished fourth and fifth grade at Paul Revere. Looking ahead to middle school, I had my heart set on Cleveland School of the Arts. I wanted so badly to go to this school because it was for kids who had talent. It incorporated performing arts, visual arts, and literary arts. My mom made some phone calls, and I was able to audition. A couple weeks later, my mom received a letter that I been accepted. I was over the moon and so happy.

After receiving the good news from the school, my mom told me that we had to take a DNA test with my dad. Since he was in prison, we had to go downtown to take it. A week later, the results came back that my dad was 99.9% my father. I would think about my dad often. We would talk on the phone every now and then, but I always wanted to meet him in person. My uncle Nate called my mom and ask my mom if he can take me to see my dad. My mom agreed. I was so excited about going to see my dad. My uncle Nate was my dad's little brother. He had a plan for how we were going to trick my dad when he came into the room. I was supposed to stand by the vending machine on the other side of the room to make him think it was just my uncle visiting. Then, Uncle Nate would spring the surprise.

The day finally came. We were on our way to Mansfield Prison. This was actually my first time ever inside a prison. I was scared and excited at the same time. I had no idea what having a dad meant and I did not know how the visit would go. My dad was coming through the door. He was super tall, lanky, and light-skinned. I definitely got my complexion from my mom and my height from my dad. I tried not to look at him when I was standing by the vending machine, but he took one look at me and says, "Come over here, girl. Y'all can't fool me." I just started laughing, and he gave me the biggest hug. He literally took me right off my feet. That was a very special moment for me. My dad had a thousand questions to ask and I answered all of them without hesitation. I wanted to tell him everything. I remember my uncle Nate sitting there with a big Kool-Aid smile on his face. I could tell he was excited about me meeting my dad for the first time. I was just as excited as he was, and smiling just as big. My only memories of my dad before this had come from pictures and stories from my aunt and uncles. Finally, I was getting the chance to know my dad for myself, and it was just what I needed. We had a great visit and, when it was time to leave, he promised to call me from time to time.

My uncle Nate was always the one keeping me in the loop about what was happening on my dad's side of my family. Most of my family on my dad side was from Toledo, Ohio. I looked forward to the times Uncle Nate would pick me up to go to our family gatherings in Toledo.

My favorite time of the year was Kwanza. I enjoyed lighting the candles and eating all the different kinds of food. I enjoyed the laughter and getting hugs from my uncles and aunties. I had a favorite aunt from my dad's side, my Aunt Earlean. She was something special. She was outspoken, charismatic, and loving. Every other Christmas, she would send me an African Barbie doll. I looked forward to that. Her gift meant a lot to me because I knew that none of my cousins would have one. Every time I talked to her, she would remind me, "Girl, I named you." She always made me think that my name was special. I would purposely write my name over and over because I felt my name was special too.

School #6

The summer ended and it was time to start school. I couldn't believe I was going to Cleveland School of the Arts. I enjoyed music class, except the part when we had to read music. Just give me a microphone and a beat, and I was cool with that. This school was a big deal in Cleveland and I felt so important every morning while walking in the building.

My mom started acting strangely again. She sat me down and told me we might be moving again, because she needed to get some help. This time, I was old enough to know that she wasn't sick with a cold. It was from drugs and alcohol. I was thinking in my head, *Every time things are finally going good for me, I look around and I have to move.* She asked me if I wanted to go back with my aunt Jeanette and I said no. I wanted to go to my other aunt, my mom's baby sister, aunt Pam, because I admired her lifestyle. She had a big house, and it seemed that my cousins were always having fun.

My mom called my aunt and she said yes, I can go to live there. So, my big sister went back to my grandma's house and I went to my aunt Pam's. We had so much fun over there. My aunt would play favorites between us cousins from time to time, but I was still happy to be there. I know my aunt was doing the best she could with three kids of her own, myself, and a full-time daycare to manage. Even though living at my aunt's seemed fun, things were starting to change for me. Everything had started off well at Cleveland School of the Arts, but I had no structure anymore, and I started slacking in my classes. Everything was happening so fast. I was not the same girl I was when I lived with my mom. I started skipping school, smoking weed, and being around my cousins, who were in high school. I didn't have any interest in anything anymore because I found myself missing my mom. I missed that structure she provided for me and my sister. My grades started to drop, crashing to D's, and F's. This wasn't acceptable at the school, because failing grades meant you were not academically fit to move forward. So, Cleveland School of the Arts let me go.

School #7: Depression

After I failed out of Cleveland School of the Arts, my aunt decided to let me go to school with her kids. I started going to Wilson Middle School with my cousins. The area around my new school was influenced by gangs, so I formed a gang of my own called True Red. I was really only doing it because everybody else was, and because I thought it would make me fit in. I convinced my cousin Nae Nae to be a part of it with me. We would wear our red long-sleeve shirts under our white tees. We became popular and made a name for ourselves. Some other girls at school claiming blue even called themselves True Blue after us. I had got info that the leader of their group was dealing with the same dude I liked. The first time I saw her, the energy was crazy. She looked at me with an attitude, and I looked back at her with an attitude to let her know I was nothing to be messed with. See, there was another side to me that I did not mind showing if I felt threatened or tempted. I was the outspoken one. I still had anger issues, and I didn't care if I let it out, because deep down inside I felt my life was hell any way.

One day after school, my friend got into it with one of the girls from the other side. The two of them started fighting, and the girl's friend acted like she was going to jump in the fight too. The boy I really liked was there. He told me to swing, and so I swung. I knocked the girl down to the ground. I did it because my crush was there, but also because I was loyal to my friends and family.

Once I took that swing, my life changed in the blink of an eye. I was down for anything. I'd get in a fight for any cause, no matter the consequence. All the hurt and pain from my dad being in prison and my mom going back on drugs was starting to boil over in a way I had never seen. Sometimes my cousins would act funny because of my situation. Sometimes my other family members would reject me and when I felt this rejection, I really started acting out. I didn't have the finest clothes, and sometimes I would wear the same clothes back-to-back for days. But I didn't have too much of a choice, except when I would wear my cousin's clothes.

One day I saw the girl from True Blue in the hallway picking a fight with my little cousin Nae Nae. I immediately ran over there and punched the girl in the face. The school principal, grabbed me, and I was expelled for gang-related violations. I didn't rat on the rest of my group because I didn't want all of us to go down.

I clearly still had anger issues, and it could be uncontrollable when I got upset. I stopped singing, dancing, playing basketball and volleyball. My positive behaviors were completely turned into negative ones. I found myself in a deep depression. I didn't brush my teeth or wash up for days. I remember putting on layers of clothes to hide the smell from not washing. I remember meeting the boy I liked at his friend's house. I went upstairs into one of their bedrooms, and I waited for him to come and see me in the room. He came in and was feeling on me, and I tried my best not to let it go further. Somehow, he got me to take my clothes off, and I smelled so bad. He left the room, and the guys at the house kept opening and closing the door laughing. I already knew what they were laughing at. I put on my clothes and walked out.

Walking down the street that day, I felt like the dirt on the bottom of my shoe. I never felt so low in my life. I was so embarrassed, and I never went over there again. I really started not to care about anything or anybody. I was getting myself in a lot of trouble. The attention I needed was really from my mom and dad, but since I couldn't get it from them, I started getting attention on the streets. I was thirteen when I ended up leaving my aunt's house.

I remember being so drunk one night that the police stopped me while I was walking down the street. They took me into custody, and my aunt Pam had to come and pick me up. Even though I was not living with her anymore, I could still call her knowing she would come with no problem. Another time, I remember getting into a fight with some girls, and I called my aunt and she and my cousins were right there, ready to fight with me. One thing I can say about my family is that we were always there for each other, no matter how much we didn't get along.

Since I didn't have anywhere to go at that point, I went to my big cousin Nike's house for a while. I was back with my cousin Nunu again. This guy name Will lived closed by and he enjoyed our company because we were fun to be around. Will was a little older than I was, but he liked me and he didn't care, and I didn't either. He had a car, and he liked to kick it, so we kicked it. This was the time when Project Pat and MJG was bumping. We listened to them all the time. "If you ain't from my hood, you can get from round here." That was one of my favorite songs. Me and my cousin Nunu were so wild. We used to buy Thunderbird and two twenty-five cent juices, pour out the juice, put Kool-Aid in the bottles, and mix it with Thunderbird or MD 20/20. We did it that way so my big cousin Nike and our neighbors wouldn't find out. We would sit on the stairs, laugh, and talk about people that walked pass.

I also sharpened my fighting skills this particular summer. There was this girl that lived down the walkway from my big cousin, and we did not like each other at all. I fought this girl about eight times, no exaggeration. Some fights she won and some fights I won, and then some fights were a tie. The whole apartment complex anticipated those fights. We started to build a name for ourselves just by fighting. It was crazy. I used to be so mad at my cousin Nunu because she always tried to jump in. My cousin didn't want me to lose. We always had this saying, "One fight, all fight."

The summer was almost over, and my mom had an apartment in East Cleveland, EC for short. My cousin NuNu went over there with me. My mom basically gave us the apartment. Even though I hated the fact that my mom was on drugs, I enjoyed the freedom of doing what I wanted. We met this guy named Mike, and he was much older than we were. He was the biggest drug dealer around that way. I really wanted to make some money so I would show my face on the block every day just so he would notice me. I would wear baggy jeans and tank tops just to fit in with the other homies. My cousin NuNu would make fun of me all the time because she thought the way I dressed was ugly. One night, Mike was all alone walking towards the store, and there was my chance.

"What up, Mike?"

He replied, "What's up, lil mama? What you doing out here?"

"Trying to get on," I said.

He said, "What? You really trying to make some money?"

"Hell, yeah. It's hard out here!"

He told me to meet him at the apartments across the street in an hour.

I agreed, "Bet."

I was so freaking nervous. I didn't know how this was about to turn out. I didn't know if he was about to give me a lecture because I was so young or what. I rang the doorbell and this white chick answers. This female was all kinds of messed up. She was stumbling on her words and barely looking at me.

I turned to the man I'd come to see, "Mike, you gotta do better than that. This chick will get you killed."

He smiled and said, "Follow me."

Soon after, I started selling crack for him. Since I was only fourteen, I had no clue what I was doing. I just liked the title of being the only female hustler on the block. I started to notice my loyalty to the streets, and I was cool with it. I didn't have to wear the same clothes over and over again because I finally had enough money to afford more clothes.

At this point, I was not thinking about school. All I wanted to do was hustle and be in the streets. I didn't care about anything else. Later on, I found out that Mike was cheating me my money, but like I said, I had no clue what the hell I was doing at first anyway. I found this out from a good friend of mine who lived around the way. Pooh was my homie. He taught me the game. I let him cook coke in our apartment and teach me what everything would sell for. He even taught me how to drive. He used to rent my mom's boyfriend car, and we made moves together that way. I would drive Pooh all around EC. He was so cool and had mad respect for me. He never once tried to get on with me. He really treated me like his little sister. I was living an unconcerned life and with no one left to guide me, I became a product of my environment. I was selling the very thing that I had been affected by as a baby: crack.

Around this time, I also started singing again. I had a music producer. When he first came into the picture, he was producing this group called Dangerous Minds. I thought they were so raw. They went together so well. They came up with a song and wanted me to sing on the hook. Of course, I took the opportunity. "What y'all wanna do, I got my gansta crew, and we don't care so what, we just out here chopping it up with that freaky gansta style, niggas don't know that we coming wild, so please don't mess with us cause y'all can't fuck wit us." That was my part in the song while they rapped the verses. I enjoyed singing that hook because every word matched my lifestyle.

We recorded the track and it sounded so good. The group ended up parting ways due to some personal issues, but I stayed, hoping my producer would stand by his word. I had formed a bond with him and his wife. They kind of knew my situation, and I would stay at their place sometimes. I really had faith in my producer. I thought I could get a record deal. We went to New York to pass out tracks for people to hear us, but he didn't have anything set up. He rented a limo one time, and we went on Browning to drive by my grandma's house. I guess he wanted to convince my family that he was about the right thing, but down the road they knew he was full of it. He had me scuffing up money to do different things, but nothing was getting done. Eventually, I stop working with him.

School #8

When I stopped working with my producer, I gave up music. I still had my juvenile case pending for gang related violence. I knew I had to take care of that, so I moved out of East Cleveland and back in with my aunt Jeanette. She had gotten married and we called her husband "Stan the Man." I was so happy to be with my aunt again. My aunt and her husband made things real cozy for me. I remember Stan spent hours putting an entertainment center together for my room. I thought that was dope.

My aunt went to court with me and the judge said I had to go to an alternative school to get my behavior together. I fought it at first, but my aunt talked some sense to me, and I signed up to attend the program at the YMCA, which was an alternative school for troubled kids. I had to go to the program in order to get back into regular school. There were about 12 of us in the class. We were all there for different reasons, but our instructor made it work. It was more like a group therapy session in class throughout the week. Even though I hated the program, I completed it.

School #9

I transferred to Hamilton Middle School, which was down the street from my aunt Jeanette's house. I really wanted to prove to myself and to my aunt that I was going to do better, so that's what I did. Meanwhile, my aunt Jeanette and her husband started getting into it because she would be out all-night. My aunt was still struggling with her drug addiction and Stan did not agree with my aunt smoking. She ended up leaving him and eventually I had no choice but to leave their house as well. I moved in with my Uncle for a while. Then I moved in with one of my friends. My friend was so down to earth. She knew my situation and took me in as her own.

I was in the eighth grade that year at Hamilton. I was super excited about graduating onto high school, And I decided to have a graduation party at my friend house. It was lit. All my friends from my school and all my homies were there. I had a close friend who lived down the street. We were the only females in our group of friends. We used to go to the bando, smoke weed and freestyle all the time. I didn't know how to rap, but when I smoked weed, I felt like I was the best rapper alive!

School #10

My mom and her boyfriend decided to move to Decatur, Georgia, and asked me if I wanted to go with them. I said yes. It was hard to say goodbye to my friends. I don't know how many times I thanked my friend for letting me stay with her. We exchanged hugs and kisses, and then I was on my way to Decatur. I started going to Avondale High School in Georgia, but that didn't last too long. After four months, we were back in Cleveland. I had a little to do with us moving back to Cleveland because I was homesick and I couldn't get over that hump.

School #11

Back in Cleveland, I started going to East Tech High School. At this point, I was just going with the flow. I started to feel numb to moving so much because my mom couldn't stay in one spot. I was only at this school for three months before my mom moved us again. Since my mom was still doing drugs, she moved around a lot and I had no choice but to move when she did.

School #12: Drop out

I started going to John F. Kennedy High School. The only good thing about going there was that I met my high school sweetheart, Rondell. Rondell was such a gentleman, and we became like two peas in a pod. I barely went to my classes and eventually I dropped out of school. I was so exhausted with moving that I wasn't even trying to focus on my classes at that point. Everything was starting to be a blur to me. At 15 years old, I had already been to 12 schools. I just couldn't handle it anymore.

THE MIDDLE

My first job

I was tired of being broke, so I decided to apply for a job at White Castle. A few days later, I got a call from the manager saying I got the job. I remember Ms. Jackie like it was yesterday. Ms. Jackie was the hiring manager for White Castle. She was a little short lady with an accent, and very nice. I was fifteen years old and this lady gave me a chance to work. I got my work permit from the doctor and I started my first job. I was going back and forth from my boyfriend's sister's house and my mom's apartment at that point. After completing the training for my new job, I started working the graveyard shift from 11 PM to 7 AM.

I had a really bad attitude, and I got into arguments with customers like every other day. Ms. Jackie pulled me to the side and told me that I am not going to get far in life with this sort of attitude. But since she liked me, she would give me a chance to get my act together. Even though I was not trying to hear what she had to say, I knew she was telling me the truth. And I respected her, so I listened. I worked on changing my attitude little by little. It did not happen overnight, but I was willing. Even though I struggled with a bad attitude, I became one of their best cashiers. I was always on time, I worked hard, and was available to help wherever I was needed.

It was a Monday night and a man came in looking weird. His eyes were big and he kept moving his lips, but no sound came out. I asked him, "How may I help you?" He ordered a fish sandwich. I punched in his order and raised my head to tell him the total, and that's when he put a gun to my head and told me to open the register. I kept telling him I couldn't open the register, which was true. I was so nervous I literally forgot how to open the damn register. As soon as the guy turned his head for a second, I ran to the back of the restaurant. I didn't know if he was going to shoot me or not, but I took my chance. One of my coworkers ran out the back door and never came back. Eventually I stopped working at that White Castle too.

It always seemed like just when things were going right in my life, something always got in the way. I was happy with my job, and then this happens. I tried to work after that incident but I became paranoid and nervous whenever I was behind the register and I just couldn't get my mind right, so I quit. I was back at square one, and still moving back and forth between my boyfriend's sister's house and my mom's apartment on 83rd and Quincy.

American Idol comes to Cleveland

My Aunt Pam's best friend Michelle got in touch with me one day to tell me that American Idol was coming to Cleveland. Michelle was our family's hairdresser. Whenever I would go to her shop with my aunt or cousins, she would always have me sing for her and her customers. Michelle had so much faith in me. She knew I didn't have any money, so she took me downtown to Tower City and bought my outfit for my audition.

American Idol was holding open auditions at the Indian's baseball field. We had to be there hours before it started. We decided to get there ten hours early. Michelle made us sandwiches. She brought a cooler full of juice and snacks. She made sure we were all set. There were hundreds of people waiting for this opportunity. I decided to sing "Respect" by Aretha Franklin. When my number was called, I nervously went onto the field. I gave it all I had, but it wasn't enough for the judges and they said no. I was sad all that day. I really thought I had it.

I didn't have any money or anything and I really wanted to ask Michelle if I can live with her just to avoid going back to that apartment my momma had on Quincy, but I never got up the nerve to ask her. My momma was still in the streets and I made my own decisions. I tried selling crack again, but that didn't last because I smoked too much weed. Then I found out I was pregnant. I was not ready for a baby. This just stacked the odds even more against me. My momma got a check every month, which helped out a little, but I was tired of the way my life was headed. If I wasn't fighting, I was smoking or drinking—real talk.

I was still going over to my grandma's house to spend time with the family from time to time. Even though Grandma used to cuss us out, that never stopped us from going over there. My cousins and I would play cards, crack jokes, laugh, argue—you name it. Grandma's house kept us together. Going back to my mom's apartment was so depressing. She was barely there, and when she was there, we didn't spend time together because she was too busy getting high or entertaining her company. I was 16 and found myself telling God, "I hate you." I was mad at God because of my unstable life. All I ever wanted was a normal life. But when things were going halfway right, something would always happen.

Stillborn

Several months went by, and I was already six months pregnant. While lying in my bed I kept feeling pressure at the bottom of my stomach. I told Rondell to call the ambulance. I could hardly walk and I was in so much pain. I knew something wasn't right. We got to the hospital and they took me to labor and delivery. While doing my ultrasound, I could see my baby boy, but he was not moving. I kept asking the doctors what was going on. Why isn't my baby moving? Why can't I hear his heartbeat? Another doctor came in the room and told me that he was sorry, but the baby had died.

My heart dropped. I was in total shock. After going through the protocols of getting my son out, I held my son's lifeless body for hours. The doctors didn't know what caused his death, and they performed a lot of tests trying to figure it out. My heart was crushed. I was depressed for months, and all I wanted to do was drink and smoke. After my son's funeral, my relationship with my boyfriend started going downhill. I don't think my boyfriend understood my depression. We were getting into arguments and fights like every other day. Things were getting out of hand, and pretty soon we broke up for good.

Pursuing my education

My friend Nicole introduced me to Bryant and Stratton College. I was so discouraged about school at this point because I was a high school drop-out, but Bryant and Stratton had this program for people who didn't have a high school diploma. If you passed the academic test, you could take college classes while pursuing your GED. It sounded good, but I was so nervous about this. Nicole was already a student there and she encouraged me to take the test.

The school gave people three tries to pass, and if you couldn't pass it on the third try, the opportunity would be gone. The first time I failed and became discouraged. The second time I failed again by just a few points, and I really became discouraged. At this point I was ready to give up. I felt so dumb. The school didn't hear from me for a couple weeks, and then one of the admission reps called me. I told her that I don't think I could pass. She politely said, "Then what is there to lose?"

Thriving Moment

I thought about it and I decided to go in and take the test one last time. I was so nervous while waiting for my results. Some minutes later, the lady came in with a big smile and told me I had passed. I couldn't believe it. I called Nicole and told her I had passed. I was so proud to be starting school, but not just any school—I was starting College. I decided to pursue my Associates degree in Associates of Applied business, Administrative Assistant. I knew I struggled in math, so I signed up for Seeds of Literacy to get tutored for my GED. Seeds of literacy was a free program for people that needed help with passing the GED test. A lot of my peers were getting fake high school diplomas, but it wasn't in me to cheat. *I preferred earning my GED because I knew I would appreciate it more.* I wanted this more than anything. I took the GED test three times before passing because math was so difficult for me, but I pushed myself, kept getting tutored and finally got my GED. I wanted to give up plenty of times, but I stayed focused. Little by little, my focus on school were taking my mind off the loss of my son and the loss of my relationship with my ex.

I was back living with my aunt Jeanette now. I was going out frequently and spending more time with my family. I met this guy that sold weed in the neighborhood. I met him through my aunt, and he became my weed man. We became friends. I liked him because he had ambition. He was funny and charming and well-mannered. He told me his reasons for hustling, that he wanted to make enough money to get out the hood to pursue his own business and provide for his family. I told him my hustle was to finish college and get a good job. Since we knew each other's hustles, we got along very well. We supported each other and became inseparable. He was tired of living in and out of his mom's house, and he could tell that I was tired of living this way too. So, he decided to pay for an apartment for us.

The chemistry between us was amazing, and so we just let good things happen. The Veterans Affair Medical Center had a program for college students. If you kept a GPA of 2.5 or higher, you were eligible to work part-time there while going to school. I applied and got a temporary position in the kitchen at the Veterans Affair Medical Center on Wade Park. Then we made it official. We were boyfriend and girlfriend. Since this was my first time dating a street boy, I had some adjusting to do. I knew my boyfriend was not the most honest person in the world, but we made it work.

He knew I was raised in the streets, so I went on fighting sprees and had arguments with some females in his hood, but that was me marking my territory and he understood that too. We understood each other very well, even when others didn't. I accepted his lifestyle and he accepted everything about me. I knew my position, and I played it well, considering the damn headache I got from it.

Pregnant

Then, I found out I was pregnant. My boyfriend knew I was so nervous about my pregnancy because of what had happened to my son and he supported me with everything. He would take me to school and work. He made sure I was secure. Then, my boyfriend got caught with a gun in his car. I was five months pregnant and going nuts because I was doing everything on my own, from hiring a lawyer to going to school and working. We went to court thinking he would get probation but the judge sentenced him to three years in federal prison.

All I did was cry. I just couldn't wrap my head around the fact that my boyfriend was going to jail. Even though I once said I hated God, I asked for forgiveness because I needed to lean on Him. My boyfriend and I started going to church. He was going to church in prison and I was going to The Word Church off Lee Rd. We both got baptized. We were both trying to stay as positive as we could in our situation. I was so proud of my boyfriend because he got his GED while he was in prison and he was making changes to better himself.

A few months went by and it was time to have my baby shower. Our family's baby showers were not your average baby shower—they were parties. We played games and laughed. I cried because I missed my boyfriend so much, but my family made sure I didn't stay sad for long. We listened to music, and I showed off the baby gifts. My cousin Tma brought a beautiful cake printed with a picture of me and my boyfriend from one of his visitations. It was the picture of him holding my belly and kissing me on my cheek at the same time. I loved that picture.

Even though my boyfriend couldn't be there, it was still a great year because It was the year Barack Obama got elected president. Since I was considered high-risk after losing my son during my last pregnancy, the doctors kept a close eye on me. I was tired all the time from being pregnant. My colleagues and classmates could tell I was tired and they helped me a lot. I got help with tying my shoes, holding my books, and doing my homework. I had a good support system from my school. I had one final due the week before the doctors were going to induce my labor. I was so eager to graduate that I got through my final that Friday, and I ended up going to the hospital that Monday.

My baby girl is born

My mom and her husband were there. Yes, *husband*. She and her boyfriend had finally gotten married. My cousin Nunu was there too. I was so nervous. It was time. My cousin had one leg and my mom had the other. When I heard my baby cry, it melted my heart. I literally forgot all about the pain. She was six pounds and six ounces and 19 inches. She had a head full of hair. I named her Mo'Nyra Lanique Watkins. I finally got the chance to talk to my boyfriend and we both were so happy.

With my new baby girl, I decided to move in with my friend Nicole and her mom. Since I was so close to graduating, I thought it was best to live with them. I didn't want any distractions. The New Year was approaching, and every New Year's Eve my Aunt Jeanette would get on her knees and pray into the new year. For the first time, I joined her. Usually, I would have been at somebody's club or at somebody's house party, but I shocked us both and got on my knees with her. I was so thankful to make it another year. I was also thankful to be graduating soon.

Graduating college

Thriving Moment

Everything was looking up for your girl. It was finally time to graduate. I became so nervous and anxious. I looked in the crowed, and there stood my mom with my baby girl, my Aunt Earlean and her husband. The lady said my name and I stood up to cross the stage. I wanted to do my Tyra Banks walk, but I behaved and accepted my degree with the utmost professionalism. My aunt took the best pictures. Even though I had a five-month-old baby and my baby daddy was in jail, I had still pushed myself. The odds were against me, but I found the strength to beat the odds. No matter how ghetto I was, I decided I wanted more out of life.

Mom goes to prison

My mom was having major issues with her husband. He was tired of dealing with her drug addiction and it got to the point that he lied to the police. He told the police that she put a gun to his head and stole his car. They took her to jail, and then he bonded her out because he probably felt guilty for lying. On his way home from the bond lender, he had a heart attack behind the wheel and hit a pole and died. This all happened within minutes. It hurt me to tell my mom her husband was dead, and I felt so bad for my mom.

She called from the county jail to tell me she was ready to be picked up. We headed straight to the hospital. After his funeral, I could tell my mom was out of it. All she did was drink, and she barely slept. Then my mom was sentenced to three years in prison for something she didn't do. Since her husband was dead, he couldn't testify to the truth. My mom had priors on her record, so the judge made the decision based on that and what her husband's family told the prosecutor. This was a total shock. It laid heavy on my heart for days, but I had to keep going because my baby was depending on me.

I started selling drugs again to keep us afloat. I knew a couple of my boyfriend's customers and had a few of my own. Food stamps weren't enough for me and my baby. I still had to buy diapers, clothes, and other necessities. One day, my friend Nicole's mom invited me to church. I really didn't want to go because of how I was living, but I went anyway. When I got there, it seemed like Pastor Vernon was talking to me. He stepped on every one of my toes that night. He talked about everything a young girl my age could possibly struggle with: sex, drugs, money, insecurities, father issues, mother issues. I had just made $50.00, and I already only had $25.00 in my pocket. I gave the church all my drug money. My mind changed quickly. I called my main customer, gave her all my drugs, and I told her I was turning my life around. She was a good person, and she empathized with me. No matter what I went through, I always came across good people, even if they were addicts. They were still good people to me. The best people I've met came from the streets.

I would attend church frequently hoping it would take my mind off things. I was still looking for a job, and I finally got a call from one of the temp agencies I had signed up with. It was a personal assistant position, and I took it. I decided to move in with my aunt Renee because I wanted a more structured environment for my new start. My aunt Renee was my mom's little sister on her dad's side, and my mom's aunt on her mom's side. I know that seems wrong, but it's accurate. My Grandma Virg and my great-grandma had babies by the same man, which meant my aunt Renee was my mom's sister and my mom's aunt. This meant my aunt Renee was my aunt and my great-aunt. I didn't understand it for years, but that's what it was.

Making wise decisions was important to me because I now had a baby to live for. We got help from the church. They gave us a crib. I started praying every night. I was reading my Bible every day. I even joined the church choir. I had a good job. I was blessed. My aunt taught me how to budget, and I started saving towards getting my own place. I would go visit my mom in prison every chance I got. I realized I was writing my mom, dad, and boyfriend all at the same time, but I knew they needed my support. It was tough being the backbone, but who else was going to be there for my family? I put my problems aside and supported my parents and boyfriend the best way I could.

Bobby Jones comes to Cleveland

I was singing again. I was still in the choir and I was taking singing lessons from our choir director. My mind was opening up to different ideas and I started writing music again. I was able to get a few instrumentals to write to. I auditioned for the Bobby Jones competition and this time I got picked. Bobby Jones was a known gospel singer and hosted a TV program that propelled new gospel artists. I was super excited. I picked one of the songs I had written called "Go Hard." I practiced every day. I had good support. The day of the competition, my cousins, aunts, and supervisors all showed up to support me. My cousin Tma had a poster with my face on it. I thought that was really dope. I got up on stage and gave it all I had, but it was not enough for Bobby Jones. I did not get picked that day, but I wasn't sad like I was the day I didn't get picked for American Idol because I felt it was a great event and I had gotten a great experience out of it.

Recovering from grief

I decided to take a grief recovery class at the church. Grief recovery was designed to help people who experienced a loss. I could not believe I was doing this. When I first started grief recovery, I did not know what to expect. What I was hoping to heal from was the pain of my sister's separation from me. She didn't even know about my grief or my recovery. Nobody knew except the people that were in the class with me.

I was so unhappy with my relationship with my sister. We had been split up for most of our childhood and teenage years, and I really think that had a major impact on our relationship. We were totally different. Our only similarity was that we had the same mom, and I was sad about that. I couldn't vibe with my sister like I wanted to. My sister was closer with my cousins than she was to me, and seeing that made me angry and jealous. I didn't help matters that I used to call everybody and their momma "sister" more than my own sister. Every time I looked around, I was adopting somebody's daughter, or somebody's daughter was adopting me. True story. I always asked myself, how would I treat my little sister if I had one, or how would my relationship with my sister be if we had stayed together as little girls?

My sister probably didn't know this, but I admired her. She was always a hard worker, and she stayed fly. My sister stayed with the latest gear no matter what her situation was. I loved her to death, and I had to deal with the facts about our relationship. In grief recovery, our counselor asked everyone to draw a timeline of their life from childhood on up. That was so hard for me. It really brought back all the hurt and pain and separations that my sister and I went through. I can only remember me and my sister actually living together maybe five times, and each one never lasted long. While sharing my timeline with the group, I got so emotional. I didn't even realize how hurt I was from not being around my sister all those years.

I'm pretty sure my big sister was hurt in some ways too. My sister was tough, and she would shut down in a heartbeat. I just didn't want her shutting down on me. I couldn't take the rejection. In some ways, I don't think my sister knew how to be a big sister to me. I don't blame her for that at all. I just know how affected I was by it. Going to grief recovery felt good. I would usually smoke some weed and get drunk and hope all my problems would go away. But for once I decided to do something different. I went to get help, and I received it. I was still a hot mess, but I was slowly making progress.

I was also making progress in my relationship with my boyfriend. I made sure I had money on the phone to talk to him and that really helped us stay connected. My boyfriend was serving his time in Big Sandy federal prison in Kentucky. I began to plan a trip to visit him. I asked my aunt Jeanette if she would go with me, and of course she was down, like always. I couldn't believe I was about to drive to Kentucky. I loved my boyfriend so much and I wanted him to see our daughter. The day came and it was time for us to get on the road. It took us nine hours to get there, which felt like forever, but we made it. I was so nervous and scared because we were up on a hill with no stores or landmarks. There was this organization that offered shelter for families who came to visit inmates free of charge. I was so grateful for that, but uncomfortable at the same time because it was different than a regular hotel. It was country and had a smell to it, but it worked.

The next day was our visitation day, and these people at the prison gave us hell. They wouldn't let my aunt come in because they detected narcotics on her clothes. They searched my van inside out and told my aunt she had to leave. My aunt drove back to the room to wait on us there. They let me and the baby in, and I was super excited about seeing my boyfriend. The baby and I were waiting at the table and he came in. OH. MY. DAMN. He was looking so good. Fresh cut, body looking good. He was looking better than he did when we first met. We could not keep our hands off each other.

My boyfriend bonded well with our daughter and we took many nice pictures. My cheeks were hurting so bad because I couldn't stop smiling. We were so happy to be with each other. The next day, my aunt was able to visit him with us. We made sure we washed her clothes really good so the security wouldn't have anything to say when we arrived. We really enjoyed our visit. Back in Cleveland, I continued writing him and sending him pictures.

I saved enough money to finally get my own place. It only took three days to find an apartment I liked. I started buying things for my apartment, all of it cash-money. My aunt Renee was so proud of me, and I was so grateful for her. She was a kingdom woman, and she modeled that in front of me and my baby girl. All she wanted was for me to love God and get on my feet. I bought my first bedroom set with cash-money, baby! I already had a living room set from the place my boyfriend and I had. Things were great. I was working, still going to church, and still in the choir.

After one year, it was time for my boyfriend to come home. I requested the day off to go get my man. I picked him up and then we were on our way back to Cleveland. I showed him my apartment and he was so proud. Since he had to go to the halfway house, we couldn't waste too much time or he wouldn't get the chance to see his family before he went. Afterwards, I drove him to the Akron halfway house. I was so happy he chose the Akron halfway house and not the one in Cleveland, because he would have been too close to the hood. After three months in the halfway house, he was released and we decided to take it a step further and get married.

My wedding day

Here was the big day. Time was getting close. While my make-up was being done, the flower girls walked in. They were beautiful. I chose my aunt Jeanette to walk me down the aisle, and my sister was my maid of honor. They both were stunning too. After seeing how good everyone looked, I could finally breath. My make-up was flawless. I literally looked like a black Barbie doll. It was time to walk down the aisle. I looked at my aunt and she looked at me and asked, "Are you ready"? I said, "Yeah, let's do this!" I can still see all my family and friends standing there. I felt so shy in that moment. I saw my Grandma Virg sitting in the front and the two empty seats reserved for my absent parents. I started to get emotional. I looked on the other side, and I saw my boyfriend's mom and dad sitting in the front and all his side of the family. It was just like the weddings in the movies, but this was all so wonderfully real. It was time for my aunt to hand me off to my groom. He politely supported my arm, and there we were. Together. It was time to exchange vows. We hadn't rehearse anything. It was straight off the dome. He said the most beautiful words ever. We exchanged rings, kissed, and then the pastor prayed over us. I felt so loved that day.

Three Months later

I can tell it was a struggle for my husband to adjust to a lifestyle so different from what he's used to. *I could see so much more for him, but sometimes what we see for other people really doesn't matter if they don't see it for themselves.* My husband was on probation, but he just couldn't stay away from the streets. I had already done a three-year bid with him, and I had zero tolerance when it came to him going back to the hood. Little by little, he started going to the hood, and I did not like it one bit.

Then I found out I was pregnant again, and the memories from my time carrying our first daughter came flooding back. I went through so much when he went to prison and I was afraid he would leave me again. The streets already weren't a part of my life anymore, and we just had a difficult time staying on track as a couple. I couldn't force him to stay home, and a lot of my days became stressful. Then one day, I got a collect call from my husband. He had violated his probation and as a result he had to serve the rest of his time. I was already angry because he had missed the birth of our first daughter, and now this meant he would miss the birth of our second daughter as well. Even though we were not on good terms at the time, I decided to stay by his side regardless, because I honored my vows.

I started making unhealthy decisions. I moved out my apartment because I felt I couldn't do everything on my own. Then, I had the baby. I named her Tori Ann Watkins. Even though I was struggling with two babies and a husband in jail, I was still in love with my husband and I made sure I stayed in touch with him until he came home. After two years, he finally came home. Now that he was back, I made sure everything was about him. Wherever he wanted to go, we went. Whatever business he needed to take care of, we made it happen. Except for the times I had to work, our schedule revolved around him. I didn't know I had so much patience until I met this guy. When you love someone, nothing matters but that person. It doesn't even matter what they've done. What really mattered was that we were together.

While my husband served his prison time, I had matured, and I was not the same girl he met eight years earlier. I was a woman now. I had outgrown the streets, while I think he wanted me to stay the same girl I was. I tried to be that girl for him, but I was hurting myself in the process. And yet, I still forced myself to stay. I wanted our marriage to work so badly, to the point that I was willing to put up with anything. I put up with the cheating, the lies, the craziness. Then, everything I thought I could put up with suddenly became unbearable.

Shelter

I was fed up with sleeping on my mother-in-law's couch with two kids. On top of that, I was pregnant for the third time. Exhausted from the constant stress, I called Laura's Home Women's Crisis Center to see if they had a room available for me and the girls. I didn't want to move in with anybody else. When I called, the woman on the phone told me that the list changed every day, and that I would have to call every morning at 7AM in order to be added to the list. I called every day for six days. On day seven, I got a call. Laura's Home Women's Crisis Center is a shelter run through the city mission and its goal is to provide stability for women with children. I packed up only what the girls and I needed, and then I was on my way. This was very different for me and the girls, but at that point I didn't care because I needed help. I was assigned to a case manager, and she told me that I had two options going forward. Either I could continue working and get their assistance on finding a place, or I could be in their program for nine months, but I would have to quit my job in order to join the program, which was Monday through Friday from 7AM until 4PM. I chose to be in the Laura's Home program. I wrestled with the decision for a few days, but in the end, I knew that I needed help more than I needed some job. It was definitely a leap of faith. I had always worked to support me and my kids, and it was difficult admitting that I couldn't do it all alone.

After telling my case manager that I was going to stay, she told me that the welfare office had a connection with Laura's Home and that if I worked for them, I could receive a welfare check and be able to keep my food stamps. Of course, I said yes. Everything was right there for me and the girls. Laura's Home provided daycare for the girls while I went to their classes and worked. They fed us breakfast, lunch, and dinner.

My challenge with all of this was being around so many other females. We all had different personalities and were in different situations. There were days I wanted to go off and take some heads off some shoulders. I really had to adapt to the environment. I had formed a good bond with one of the staff members who worked the night shift. She was such a blessing. She would calm me down when I felt overwhelmed. I was being tested on all fronts. There were plenty of nights I wanted to pack up and leave, but I pressed through. I pressed through the negative feelings and emotions I was having towards staying. I prayed, I stayed consistent, and I was determined to get through the program.

While living at Laura's Home, I had to wake up at a certain time every day and get ready for chapel. My room had to pass inspection every morning. I started to appreciate the structure. I started to enjoy chapel because that was a place where all the women in the program came together to listen to different speakers and worship. One morning, I had a lot on my mind, and I just started singing

"Praise Is What I Do" by William Murphy. That was the first time I let anyone hear my voice at this place. I was hurting and music was my outlet.

Thriving Moment

As the days went by, I started waking up earlier and spending more time with God. I started writing and listening to my inner voice. I started praying for my kids, my family, and the women there with me. As much as I wanted to cry and sob over my situation, God did not allow that to happen. He began to use me. I was validating these women's pain even if I didn't understand it at times. The program director even gave me a platform to speak from time to time. I was starting to be a little big sister at Laura's Home. I say "little big sister" because some of the women I was helping and encouraging were much older than I was. I realized that there was purpose in my pain.

The classes at Laura's Home were amazing. Touch of Reality was the very first class I took. I began to be open up and express some of my issues. We had this one exercise that I loved so much. We had a small brown paper bag and a stack of magazines. We were to cut out pictures that we thought represented ourselves and use them to decorate and fill the bag. The picture that represented us on the inside went into the bag, and those that represented us on the outside were glued to the bag's exterior. When we finished, we presented our pictures to each other. I started from the inside of the bag because my main reason for being there was for healing and restoration. We all made some really good art.

Another class I appreciated so much which turned out to be my favorite class was Dialectical Behavior Therapy, or DBT. In DBT, we learned skills in four main areas: mindfulness, distress tolerance, emotional regulation, and interpersonal effectiveness. All four categories gave me tools to use while in stressful situations. I learned about using my wise mind and how to self-soothe when I was overwhelmed. I learned how important emotions were and how to handle them when they arose.

There was also a class on empowered relationships. This class was about domestic violence. I did not know that I was in an abusive relationship until I took this class. I always thought domestic violence had to be physical, but I found out that most domestic abuse situations involve mental or emotional, not physical, violence.

I also liked the class called Changes that Heal. This class gave me another perspective on dealing with people. I learned how to validate other people's feelings, even when I didn't agree with the way they expressed them. Validation was my favorite topic in this class because I learned that it was okay to listen and even validate myself when I felt a certain way about a certain person or situation. I learned that everyone is entitled to how they feel—including myself.

It was almost time to have baby number three. My husband couldn't be there again because he was in jail. I was kind of used to this cycle by now, and I simply did what I had to do. It was not easy preparing for another baby by myself, but I had no choice. I received help from Laura's Home volunteers. I was given clothing, diapers, bottles, and blankets. About one month later, I had the baby. I named her Naomi Marie Watkins. As I was leaving the hospital, I felt so sad because I had to drive me and my newborn home myself. Usually, people who have just had a baby have someone to drive them home, but not me. This was the second time I had to do this, and I was mentally exhausted.

A couple months later, I graduated from the Laura's Home program and got my own place.

Abortion #1

After receiving great counsel from Laura's Home, I found out I was not as strong as I thought. I became lonely with my three kids. My husband got out of jail, and I started to be around him again. A lot was happening, and one day I found myself at the abortion clinic. *What the hell was I doing there?* I thought to myself. I never understood abortions until then. I could not handle another baby because I was already struggling with the three kids I had. My husband and I agreed to the decision. I was so nervous. They put me on the table, and before I knew it, I was knocked out. I woke up to an empty room.

Abortion #2

A month went by and I was pregnant again. I decided to get another abortion. I called my aunt Jeanette and asked her if she could drive me to the clinic. I could not believe I was doing this again. I looked up to the sky, hoping I would not go to hell for this. They put me under again, and again when I woke up it was to an empty room. My relationship with my husband was not getting better. We still argued and got into fights often. It got so bad that it felt like either I was going to kill him, or he was going to kill me.

Divorced with three kids

I was not myself anymore, and I thought I was losing my mind. I couldn't think straight or hold a normal conversation with anybody. I decided to file for divorce. I told my husband everything I was doing, and he didn't even put up a fight. I think he wanted the divorce too, but he was a coward, and so he waited for me to do everything. Since this was my third attempt to divorce, my aunt Jeanette cursed me out because I couldn't make up my mind about divorcing him. I finally convinced her that this was it for me. I took a shot of Grey Goose, smoked my Black & Mild, and was on my way to the courthouse with the papers. I knew nothing about doing paperwork, and one of the ladies that worked there was very patient with me. This lady was a gift from God. She helped me with everything. She practically did it all for me except sign my name. She looked in the system to tell me when I could come to court. She paused and said, "Girl, today is your lucky day. You can come back at 1:00PM if you really want this divorce." I paused for a moment, thinking about everything that had led me to this day. I started thinking about all the years we missed together because he was in jail or on the streets. Five years, out of our eight-year relationship, he was in jail.

I started thinking about all the holidays and birthdays he'd missed. He wasn't there for any of our kids' births. All the jail visits, collect calls, letters, passenger seat rides, and three beautiful little girls were not enough for him. I started thinking about how hard I struggled to take care of myself and the girls without him. I started thinking about all the times I was with my cousins or my sister and their boyfriends, but I was alone. After thinking about all of that, I politely and boldly told the lady, okay. I would be there at 1PM. My aunt was outside with the baby waiting on me to call. I told her that we didn't have to wait for a court date. We parked and waited for the time. My paperwork was all finished, signed and notarized. There I was, standing in front of the judge with my aunt by my side and with my nine-month-old baby on my hip. We raised our right hands to affirm everything was true. There I was, divorced with three kids. *I thought I was going to be married to this man forever. I was in a mental shock, and you can tell because it was written all over my face.*

THE NEW

Delayed, but not denied

After reflecting on my life, I knew l had to make a change and I began to think about possibly joining the Army. In order to enlist in the Army, I had to take and pass the ASVAB test. I decided to take the test. The ASVAB is the Armed Services Vocational Aptitude Battery test and help you identify which Army jobs would be best for you. I failed it three times, and I became discouraged all over again. I remember when I was applying to college, and that admission rep had said, "What is there to lose?" Remembering her words gave me the strength to persevere. I studied and took as many practice tests as I could. I did finally pass the ASVAB, and then I started making arrangements. I put in my notice of resignation at the VA Medical Center where I worked at the time. My big cousin Nike was willing to look after my kids while I went to basic training. I was sworn in and, after receiving my departure date, I drove my kids to Virginia and had everything set up for their stay.

Other than my divorce, sending my kids off was the toughest decision I had to make. My girls were my everything, but I had to remind myself that they were the ultimate reason I was joining the military. I had to keep reminding myself that I was leaving them for a good cause.

I thought I was ready for Basic Combat Training, but I wasn't. All the waking up early, making up your bed a certain way, and being around all these people was crazy to me. I found myself asking the question again: *What the hell am I doing here?* I was 29-years-old, 10 to 12 years older than most of my battle buddies.

There were drill sergeants everywhere watching our every move. There were days when I just wanted to quit and go home, but once again I pressed through. I was really observant, and I decided to stay in my own lane. I was not about to try and fit in with anybody. I had done enough of that in my younger years, and it never led to anything good. I did what I was asked to do, and I went to church every Sunday. I was so happy about church because that was a day of worship for me.

Taking the physical training test was hard because I hadn't worked my muscles in years. I felt like something was wrong with my legs. I ran so slow, and at times I thought I was going to pass out on the track. I formed a bond with one of the females in my platoon. She was an excellent runner. She helped me and motivated me a lot. She was much younger than I was, so her help was much needed. I failed my first two Physical Training tests and passed the last one. I started to be pretty good at running, and when I thought of my kids, I was encouraged to push even harder.

Thriving Moment

A lot of females in my Army platoon started to draw close to me. I had some tough days, but I knew these young ladies needed to see my strength. I started to encourage them, pray for them, and talk to them when they needed someone to listen. I was far from perfect, but God used me right where I was, and eventually, they started calling me "Mama Watkins." Even the males in my platoon were calling me Mama Watkins. I was not expecting this, but I learned that it was not all about me. The same experience I had in Laura's Home was starting to repeat itself in basic training. My struggles became an inspiration to myself and those around me.

I remained solid, and I graduated basic training and AIT (Advance Individual Training). I couldn't believe I was in the Army. Looking back to when I failed the ASVAB test all those times, I would not have thought I would actually make it in the Army. It felt good to walk across that stage and walk out of the barracks. I was so grateful for my big cousin's support. They took good care of my kids while I was away. It's already hard finding a babysitter for one kid, but finding support for three was definitely a blessing.

I spent the weekend with the girls in Virginia at a hotel and told them all about my experience in basic training. I bought them whatever they wanted. I told them that my main reason for joining the military was because of them. I told them that I wanted a better lifestyle for them than what I had growing up.

It was time to get on the road to head to my first duty station. I was able to bring my two-year-old with me, but I had to wait until my two oldest finished the rest of the school year. I really missed my kids, and I was not going to be complete until I had all three by my side. I gave the girls a big kiss and told them I would be seeing them very soon.

The car GPS said it would take us one day and 13 hours to get to Fort Bliss, Texas. The car was packed, and I had just a little room for the baby car seat in the back. We made it to my first duty station at Fort Bliss and stayed in a hotel for two weeks before I found an apartment. Once I got my apartment, I made sure everything was set up for my babies to come home. I finally sent for the girls now that they were done with school. Now, finally, I was complete. I was so happy to have my babies with me at my first duty station. This was definitely a blessing. I made sure I kept my girls busy. I put my two oldest in summer camp and my youngest in daycare while I was on duty.

Then, I got a text message from this male soldier I had met two weeks prior. I had given him my number not thinking he was really going to contact me. Exchanging numbers was just something all soldiers do so I didn't think anything of it. We were in the same battalion and I think he had his eyes on me for a while. He met me at the park with the girls and we spent about an hour together. After we met up, he texted me again and said he really wanted to get to know me. I was so broken from my divorce and I really didn't want a boyfriend at that point, but he kept pursuing me and I gave him a chance. We started dating and soon made it official. We were boyfriend and girlfriend.

Then, my chain of command informed everyone that we would be deploying to Afghanistan. I was so worried. I didn't want to leave my girls again. I didn't know what I was going to do. About three weeks after finding out we was going to deploy, I went to the doctor to get my yearly check-up and found out I was pregnant. I had known there was a slight chance it could happen, but to have it really happen was crazy. I called my boyfriend and told him to meet me at my place. When I told him I was pregnant, he looked me in the eyes and said, "I will support you with whatever you want to do."

Since I was pregnant, I was told that I would not be deploying. I couldn't believe how all of this was happening. Then, I had to deal with my boyfriend leaving to Germany. I did not want to pressure him about it because I did not want to get in the way of his military career. I don't know how many times I cried when he left. There were so many emotions inside of me. I had so many emotions because my boyfriend was gone, I was pregnant while taking care of three kids and on top of that, I was pregnant while serving in the Army.

My due date was approaching and my aunt Jeanette came from Cleveland to help me. Then, I started having pain. I went to the hospital, not wanting to take any chances. The doctors kept me and I had to have a C-section. My aunt stayed with the girls, and I had my baby. Her dad named her Abigail Lia Aminata Kamara. Our baby girl weighed 7 pounds. After her birth, I was able to get three months of maternity leave. Within those three months, I was able to get my body back in shape and bond with my baby.

Pressing through

After my aunt went back to Cleveland, I learned that I needed God more than anything and anyone. Some days, I didn't know what I was going to do with four kids while serving in the Army, but I made sure I was going to do everything in my power to stay in the Army. My two oldest daughters would stay at home until I got off duty, Monday through Friday when they didn't have school, while my two youngest would go to daycare. I made sure my platoon sergeant and chain of command didn't know too much about my situation. If they had found out I didn't have someone to care for my kids, they could have discharged me, and I was not going back to Cleveland. I was a single mother doing everything I could. I knew how it was to struggle back home. I didn't want to be around the drama, the killing, and the same toxic environment. When I had 24-hour staff duty, I would leave my nine-year-old in charge. I bought a house phone and made their favorite foods. Being a single parent in the Army was tough, but I had to do what I had to do. I had mother-to-daughter talks with my oldest. I prayed over them, put my PC (patrol cap) on, and went to do my job.

Thriving Moment

I was gaining strength I never knew I had. I was starting to worry less and trust God more. I had confidence that my life was in his hands, and that whatever happened was meant to happen. I kept myself off social media and paid more attention to my goals, my book, and my kids. The pressure was real, but I kept my head up and stayed focused. I didn't understand everything God was doing, but I trusted him anyway. I started counseling sessions, and things really started getting real. My counselor was a beautiful Mexican woman of faith. I poured out my life to her. At that point, I didn't care what she thought of me. I just knew I needed help. I wasn't so independent as to think I didn't need somebody. We all need somebody. I don't care how strong you think you are.

My counselor gradually started giving me assignments to work on. She gave me assignments to work on with my kids. She gave me assignments to address areas I needed help in. She could tell I was struggling as a single mother, and she helped me. After a while of going to my counseling sessions, I noticed I was crushing each day. I was thriving in my household. I felt empowered. I wanted better for me and my kids, and I took some very important steps to get us there.

I took care of Nyree first

I realized that if I didn't give myself any attention, it was hard to give the girls the proper attention. This one particular week, it seemed like everything I was watching and reading talked about self-care. It was like God was trying to tell me to start taking care of myself. I couldn't even fathom that thought, but I knew a change had to happen. I was so used to putting myself last, I didn't even know where or how to start, so I started by just making small adjustments to my schedule. I first started waking up 45 minutes earlier to get myself showered and dressed before waking up the kids. After that 45-minute adjustment became a habit, I stretched myself a little more and started waking up one hour earlier. Instead of rushing to get into the shower, I was able to take my time, which made all the difference. Then one hour earlier became two hours earlier. Within those two hours, I was able to shower, get dress, pray, meditate, and work on completing some goals.

I felt so good having my hair done and body cleaned before waking up my kids. I had so much good energy from taking care of myself first. Have you ever heard this saying, "You can't give what you don't have?" It is *absolutely* true! When I started bathing myself first, brushing my teeth first, doing my hair first, saying positive words about myself first, that's when my whole household changed. The atmosphere shifted into something I had never seen before. I know some of you are probably thinking, *Two hours early? I could never do that.* Some of you single mommas probably work a nine-to-five and feel like you have a million other things to do on top of it, but let me be the one to tell you, if there's a will, there's a way. Since I was giving myself the attention I very much needed, I was able to be effective at doing the same thing for my girls.

I forgave myself

While making these adjustments. I had to understand that nobody is perfect. Everybody had flaws and weaknesses. I can honestly say I have done some dirt in my lifetime. I've hurt some folks, knowingly and unknowingly. I can definitely say I have hurt my kids. I've taken anger out on my kids. I remember one day whooping my daughter so badly that I cried right after. I knew something wasn't right. All I knew how to do was yell, yell, yell. I thought yelling would make them do what I wanted them to do or stop doing what I felt they shouldn't be doing.

I was infested with anger. A lot of times, my kids suffered from it. And I suffered from it, too. I would go from zero to one hundred in a snap and deal with the consequences later. That had been my way for a very long time. Sometimes, I didn't care who I offended or hurt, as long as I was getting my point across and ultimately getting what I wanted, and I would always feel guilty later on because of it. The uncontrollable bursts of rage, too often directed at my children. And a lot to do with the anger I had from childhood and the anger I had towards their dad, my ex-husband. I beat myself up so many times because I felt I had failed my kids because their dad and I were not together anymore. I felt like I had failed myself too. I blamed myself for a lot of things.

I used to hear people say, "Forgive others," but something was not adding up for me. I found myself going back to the old memories and old feelings. One day, after meditation and prayer, my inner voice said, *Forgive yourself.* I think a lot of us forget to forgive ourselves because we are so worried about other people. I truly believe that all the resentment I carried towards myself was showing through, in my behavior. I had to forgive myself for the abortions and the divorce, for hurting my kids and hurting other people. I had to forgive myself for all the times I allowed my anger to control me. I was healing myself from the disease of holding onto grudges. I faced myself for the first time. It was such a relief, just saying everything I had forgiven myself for.

Then, I went on YouTube and listened to affirmations about forgiveness. I gave myself 30 days to say these affirmations. It took about ten minutes of my day, and the best time for me was when I was in the shower. For the first week and a half or so, I had to push through the negative emotions when reciting these affirmations, but the key was consistency. I didn't skip a day or give up. I kept saying these affirmations until they became my reality. Some days I felt the opposite of what I was reciting, but I said it anyway. There were days when I just didn't want to say these affirmations, especially if I had done something I wasn't proud of that day or the day before. But I had to stop beating myself up about the small things. I had to pick myself back up and keep thriving.

I submitted to serving my children

I was that parent that needed to be in control of everything. It was my way or the highway. I was a bully in my own household. All I did was yell, fuss, and cuss to get my point across. After noticing my weaknesses, I prayed for clarity and confirmation. The old saying goes, "If you don't like something about yourself, change it." I definitely didn't like how I was treating my children, so I made up in my mind to be their servant. Now, this didn't mean I allowed my kids to walk all over me. This didn't mean I let my kids get away with everything either. I learned how to be firm while serving my children. I was ready to be the best steward over these little humans that God had blessed me with. I began to take a full inventory of my kids' behaviors. I started observing them one by one, paying closer attention to their personalities, and that was how I was able to serve them.

Mo'Nyra is the oldest and she is the computer wizard. She's my witty brainiac. Since she loves electronics, we do fun things together on the phone and computer. My second-oldest, Tori, is the dancing machine. She would dance all day if I let her, so a lot of our time together is spent playing music and dancing to our favorite songs. Naomi is my third baby. She loves to talk. This girl can talk you to sleep. I serve her by allowing her to voice her opinion. I purposely let her lead the conversation. She is a boss in her own world. And baby Abigail is the youngest. She has lots of humor. She would laugh at anything. The most precious thing about her is when she puts her hand over her face and laughs. I always thought that was so cute. I serve her by always acting silly with her, even if that meant me making funny faces or weird noises. I make sure I enjoy serving my girls without putting pressure on myself.

I set a daily schedule for my household

Being a single mother in the military was not easy, but without a schedule, life was even tougher. I was blessed to have the experience of both being a working mom and a stay-at-home mom, thanks to COVID-19. When I say I know the struggle, I know the struggle. And when I say I am living proof that you can thrive while being a single mother, I mean that too. You really can do just that.

I used to be the queen of excuses until I got tired of being miserable. I knew I was all over the place, so I had to create a schedule for myself and the girls. What I learned from being a working mom and a stay-at-home mom was that I needed a schedule in both positions. Structure was essential if I wanted to thrive throughout my day.

Here was my schedule when I was serving in the military:

4:00AM – Brush my teeth, wash my face, and put on PT uniform

4:30AM – Make baby bottles and wake baby up

5:00AM – Get baby dressed and get toddler dress

5:30AM – Leave the house to drop off the younger kids

5:50AM – Drop kids off at daycare

6:15AM – Formation and salute the flag

6:40AM – Start PT

7:30AM – Head home to "conduct hygiene maintenance" (take a shower) and eat breakfast

9:00AM – On duty

5:00PM – Off duty and head to pick girls up from daycare

5:30PM – Head home

6:00PM – Cook dinner and feed the girls

7:00PM – Put girls in the tub

8:00PM – Put girls in bed

8:15PM – Push-ups, sit-ups, and planks

8:30PM – Take a bath and brush teeth

9:00PM – Stretch, meditate, and pray

9:30PM – Write

10:00PM – Sleep

Here was my schedule for the six months I stayed at home:

5:00AM – Pray, meditate, and stretch

5:30AM – Take dog out

5:40AM – Run or workout for 45 minutes

6:30AM – Shower and get dressed

7:30AM – Breakfast for the girls

8:00-9:30AM – Learning time for toddlers and school for the older girls

10:00AM – Playtime outside

11:00AM – Lunch

12:00PM – Reading time for the girls while babies nap

3:30PM – Snack

4:00-5:30PM – Family time or free time

5:30PM – Dinner

6:30PM – TV time

7:30PM – Bath for everyone

8:30PM – Bed for girls

9:00PM – Shower for myself

9:30PM – Me time

10:30PM – Bed for myself

I have my schedule in place to keep me on my toes. I make sure I set my alarm for everything that needs to be done. My alarm is my reminder, especially when I get lazy. There are days when I just don't feel like getting ready for my day, but I push through it and my routine becomes a habit.

I also give my kids responsibilities according to their ages. First, I ordered a meal chart from Amazon. It had breakfast, lunch, and dinner from Monday to Sunday. I put what food we were going to eat and the time each meal would be served. I feel so good looking at my meal chart. It gives me something to look forward to three times a day. It is a pretty cool organizational tool. Secondly, I was able to add chores on the chart for the oldest girls to do. One washes dishes one day, while the other sweeps the floors and wipes down the tables and countertops. They switch every day, so neither feels like she was doing more than the other. Even my four-year-old has a responsibility. She has to make her bed every morning and keep her room clean. And of course, the big girls have to keep their rooms clean as well.

I created a balance

I was starting to be my biggest cheer leader. Since I had a pretty good schedule in place, I decided to go on a spiritual journey. I detoxed from everything. When I say everything, I mean everything. I wanted to hear what my spirit had to say.

Spiritually, I wasn't listening to anything but spiritual instrumentals and motivational speeches on YouTube.

Physically, I started to pay attention to what I was putting in my body, so I began to eat less meat and exercised more. Eventually, I was eating 80% fruits and veggies and 20% meat. Mentally, I controlled my thoughts by meditating. I focused on keeping concentration. Emotionally, I allowed myself to be vulnerable again. Financially, I started spending my money wisely by minimizing fast food and unnecessary spending. I was in tune with myself. I was in tune with my spirit.

I remember people used to say, "Fake it till you make it," but that statement is very misleading because I always found myself dealing with those same mountains. So, I came up with a new saying: "Face it till you make it." I learned to face everything head on, instead of acting like something I'm not. I learned so much about myself in this transition, in facing myself and my reality. I realized that I was not a religious person. I detoxed from religion, and I let go of old theologies that I grew up on and focused on my reality. I used the discipline I learned from church and the military and applied it. This was my metamorphosis. I could finally hear my thoughts. I hadn't felt that free since I was ten years old performing on Showagon. I realized that I was a spiritual being having a human experience.

After experiencing my spiritual awakening, I began to change my energy. I was my own thermostat. I began to manage my anger by taking deep breaths, by meditating, and by working out. I created balance in my music. I enjoyed all kinds of music, including R&B, rap, gospel, and jazz. I made sure I did not corner myself in any type of way. I was free as a bird. I made sure I gave some attention to myself, some attention to my kids, and some attention to my goals. I worked hard and I saw great results. Having a balance in my home was the icing on the cake!

Lessons

When I was a little girl and I heard certain family members saying negative things about me and my mom, I let them shape how I thought about myself for a long time. But I later learned a lesson and that was to never let other people's opinions of me become my reality.

When I was homeless all those times and going to all those different schools, I learned a lesson then too. And that lesson was to make sure I created stability for me and my kids, because I learned by experience that a child's environment determines the structure of their life. And since I've learned that lesson, I bought my first home at 32 years old. I made sure my kids would never experience what I went through, the homelessness, the instability, and the uncertainty.

What I learned from my divorce was to never marry potential, marry reality. I learned to never use loyalty as an excuse to stay in bondage.

What I learned from being a single mother is that when things get hard, go harder. I learned to never use my kids as an excuse to do nothing.

When I went on my spiritual journey, I learned yet another lesson, and that was to include God in everything I do. Even though my spiritual journey was enlightened, I tried to do it without God, and I didn't get my full blessing until I acknowledged who He was in my process.

What I didn't know was that every lesson I learned came with a bag of blessings too. I needed every lesson in order to handle the blessings in store for me.

Thriving on purpose

Now that you know my story, hopefully you don't have to feel alone in yours. Sometimes, we don't know how strong we are until we are put in situations where we have no other option except to endure. You are stronger than you think. I always thought I was not qualified enough to be successful because I was born a crack baby. I really thought my anger issues disqualified me from being used by God. But that's when He used me the most—*in my struggle*. While other people were writing me off, God was rewriting my story.

I was a crack baby with issues, and God still saw purpose in me. My parents were out of my life for a very long time, and God still saw purpose in me. I was abandoned and rejected, and God still saw purpose in me. I was a very unstable baby, teenager, and young adult, and God still saw purpose in me. God is strategic in all he does, and he picks and uses and finds purpose in the people that others think aren't good enough. I really thank God for putting his super on my natural because without him, I know for certain that I would not have gotten through some of the things I've been through to be here today. I would have been one of those "would've, could've, and should've" people.

I am no longer confirmed by the things of the world anymore. I am confirmed by the God in me. God has already given me everything I need on the inside. It is ultimately up to me to dig deep within myself, to listen to my inner voice, and to be led by it.

You've got what it takes to succeed in raising your children. You don't have to let your past situations define your future. When raising my kids, I often felt defeated because I made so many mistakes from lack of experience. If you are a single parent and you feel defeated, I encourage you to turn that defeat into determination and let your babies be your motivation. That's what I had to do. I couldn't sit in self-pity any longer because I would not have gotten anything done. I would have just made excuses. We have to stop making excuses, and instead make adjustments. Yes, I know it's hard sometimes, but that's when you go harder.

I realized that I wasn't just setting the tone for me, I was also setting the tone for my daughters. I used to be so upset about raising my girls on my own, but there was purpose in raising my kids, and there still is. From motherhood to sisterhood, it all has purpose. From scars to pain, it all has purpose.

When I was in college, I had a purpose. My purpose was to show my colleagues, friends, and loved ones the strength behind my pregnancy. While going through college pregnant, I didn't see my purpose, but now I see it so clearly.

When I was in the shelter, I had a purpose. My purpose was to give other single mothers hope in the struggle.

Serving in the Army, I had a purpose. My purpose was to be the backbone for my battle buddies, even if I had to sacrifice my own feelings at times. My purpose was showing other single soldiers with children that it's possible to serve while raising your kids.

In raising my girls, I have a purpose. My purpose is to give them hope by being the best version of myself.

My purpose for writing this book is to let you know that you can thrive in your struggle. It doesn't matter how your life started. What matters is how you finish. I embrace my struggles. And when I wake up every day, I look myself in the mirror, and I tell myself, "Thrive on, Momma!"

Printed in the United States
by Baker & Taylor Publisher Services